The Mysterious Musical Day

Sheri Calhoun

TEACH Services, Inc.
P U B L I S H I N G
www.TEACHServices.com • (800) 367-1844

Copyright © 2021 Sheri Calhoun
Copyright © 2021 TEACH Services
ISBN-13: 978-1-4796-1168-3 (Paperback)
ISBN-13: 978-1-4796-1169-0 (ePub)
Library of Congress Control Number: 2021909539

All scripture references are taken from the King James Version (KJV) of the Bible. Public domain.

Illustrations inspired by Richard T. Williams

For my brother, Dean, and his wife, Myrtle

Published by

TEACH Services, Inc.
P U B L I S H I N G
www.TEACHServices.com • (800) 367-1844

The year was 1964. The Civil Rights Movement was deeply affecting the entire world. I was four years old at the time, and living way up north in Philadelphia, Pennsylvania. I don't remember much of what was happening in the Civil Rights Movement because my brothers and I were very sheltered and protected by my parents. I didn't know too much about what was going on outside of my home, but what I do remember is starting kindergarten that year at Larchwood Seventh-day Adventist Elementary School in West Philadelphia.

"I love school," I told anyone who would listen. School was so much fun for me. I loved to read, and I read every book on the shelf in my classroom. My teacher, Mrs. Jesse Wagner, had to send my father to the store to buy me more books to keep challenging me. What I loved reading most was the *Junior Guide*! Since it was supposed to be above my reading level for my age, I had to borrow it from my older brothers.

We read quietly during church service preliminaries every Sabbath in church. After quickly devouring my *Primary Treasure*, I turned to the *Junior Guide*. I enjoyed reading from cover to cover the stories it contained. The Bible story and Sabbath School lesson about how the children of Israel wandered around in the wilderness, told of how God supplied three weekly miracles every single week, all connected to the Sabbath and manna, bread from heaven, that He sent to feed them for forty years while they were in the wilderness.

First, they could only gather a daily portion. Anything left overnight would be spoiled the next morning all throughout the week. Next, on Friday, the day to prepare for the Sabbath, they were allowed to gather a double portion—and it wouldn't be spoiled on Sabbath morning! Last of all, no manna fell on the Sabbath day! God created the seventh day as a part of the weekly cycle in Genesis 2:2. "And on the seventh day God ended his work which he had made; and he rested on the seventh day from all his work which he had made."

Wow! I thought, God really wants the seventh-day Sabbath to be a special day, I thought. "And God blessed the seventh day, and sanctified it: because that in it he had rested from all his work

"Why do so many people go to church on Sunday?" I asked my parents. "Is it possible to change the day that God sanctified?"

which God created and made" (Gen. 2:3). This got me thinking, "Why do so many people go to church on Sunday?" I asked my parents. "Is it possible to change the day that God sanctified?" Actually, no, I was told.

Remember the story of Daniel in the lion's den in Daniel 6? He was thrown into a den of lions because he would not go along with the king's worship laws. But Daniel was not harmed, and in the end, Daniel said, "My God hath sent his angel, and hath shut the lions' mouths, that they have not hurt me" (Dan. 6:22).

"So, God's laws don't change?" I demanded.

"No, the book of Malachi, chapter 3 and verse 6 says, "For I am the Lord, I change not." The explanation continued, "When we worship God, and how we worship God is very important to God."

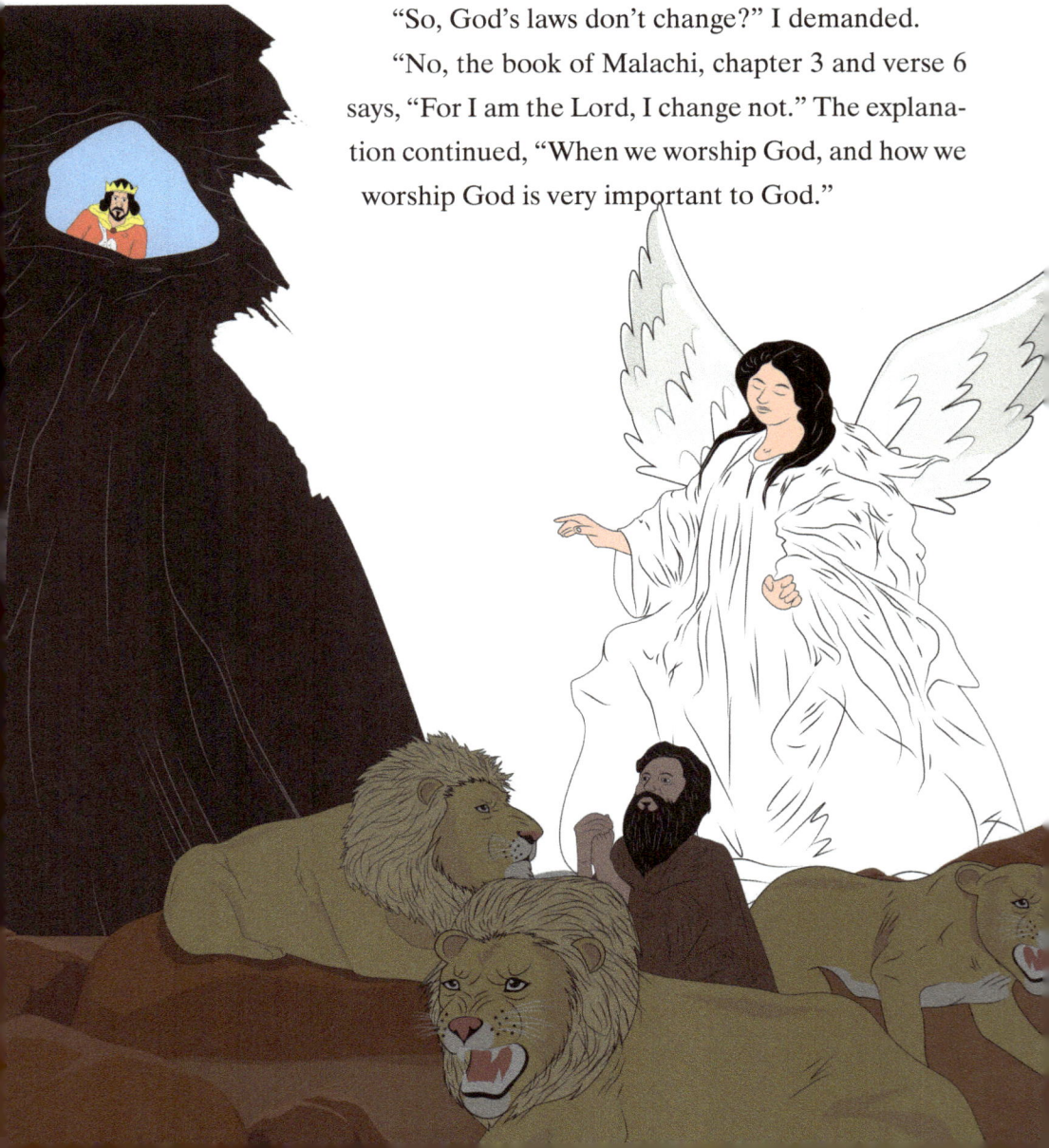

Daniel had three friends, but the king changed their Hebrew Names that had Godly meanings to heathen names, to try to brainwash them into serving his gods. For example, Daniel, which meant "God is my judge," was changed to Belteshazzar, which referred to a Babylonian god as protection.

Hananiah meant "God is gracious," which was changed to Shadrach. Mishael meant "Who is what God is?" and was changed Meshach, and Azariah meant "God has helped," which was changed to Abednego. King Nebuchadnezzar replaced God in all of their names with the names of different Babylonian gods along with the rest of the meaning of their names.

Daniel, a favorite of the king (see Daniel chapters 1 and 2), was believed to be sent out of town at the time of the fiery furnace story (below). He was about eighty years old when he was tested on the issue of worship and thrown into the lion's den. However, the three Hebrew boys were all tested on the issue of worship, too, (And I believe this has end-time applications and we all will be tested on the issue of worship, especially regarding our day of worship—Sabbath.)

In Babylon, King Nebuchadnezzar made a huge golden image, ninety feet high and nine feet wide. He commanded everyone to bow down and worship this image because the image represented him, and he wanted to be worshipped. The story, found in the third chapter of Daniel, tells how the king was furious when they would not bow down and worship this image. The king had them thrown into a fiery furnace. But remember, everyone "saw these men, upon whose bodies the fire had no power, nor was the hair of their heads singed, neither were their coats changed, nor the smell of fire had passed on them" (Dan. 3:27).

The king really liked these young adults; they worked right in the court of the king. He even gave them a second chance before he threw them into the fiery furnace. "Nebuchadnezzar said, I'll give you one more chance to demonstrate your loyalty to Babylon. When you hear the sound of the trumpets, flutes, lyres, zithers, harps, and other instruments, you had better fall to your knees and bow in worship to my golden statue. If you don't, I'll have all three of you thrown into this blazing fiery furnace. No one, not even your God, can stop me" (Dan. 3:15, Blanco, The Clear Word). The king used music to try to get these three young men to bow down and worship his image. They had all of the instruments playing "worldly music" to help persuade them to bow down and worship the golden image.

All music has a very powerful influence on our emotions, our feelings, our brains, and our bodies, and King Nebuchadnezzar knew it could be used for evil purposes. Just like he changed all of their names to represent his gods, he was intentional in adding music to his "bowing down"

or worship ceremony. The opposite is also true, and music can be used as a sweet, holy influence in church worship services and praise, to draw us closer to God.

Lucifer, the choir director in heaven, is now "the god of this world, [who] hath blinded the minds of them which believe not, lest the light of

the glorious gospel of Christ, who is the IMAGE of God, should shine unto then" (2 Cor. 4:4).

My parents surrounded us with Godly music in order to teach all of their five children the Godly purposes and influences of music. Music? Yes, I loved music as a child! Before I went to kindergarten, my mother taught me how to read music. The notes in the spaces are F-A-C-E, and the lines are E-G-B-D-F. "Just remember FACE and Every Good Boy Deserves Fudge," she encouraged.

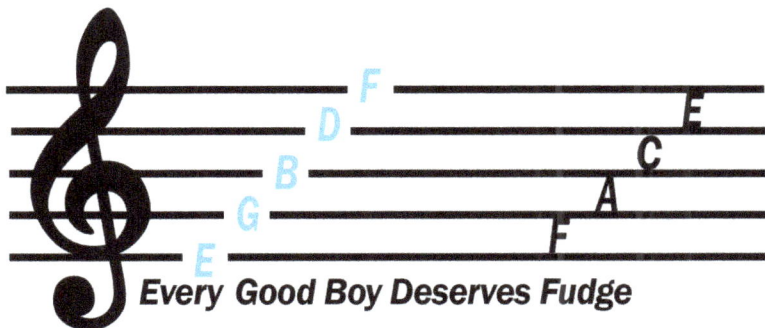

Every Good Boy Deserves Fudge

Every Sabbath morning, we attended the "Mother Church" in the city. Why was it called the mother church? Because every other church in the city began when its members went into other parts of the city and won others to Jesus, and new churches sprung up all over the city. At this church, Ebenezer Seventh-day Adventist Church, music was a solemn and sacred part of the church service. Two very talented musicians, Allen Foster, the organist, and his wife, Gwendolyn, the choir director, made music sound as if it came directly from heaven!

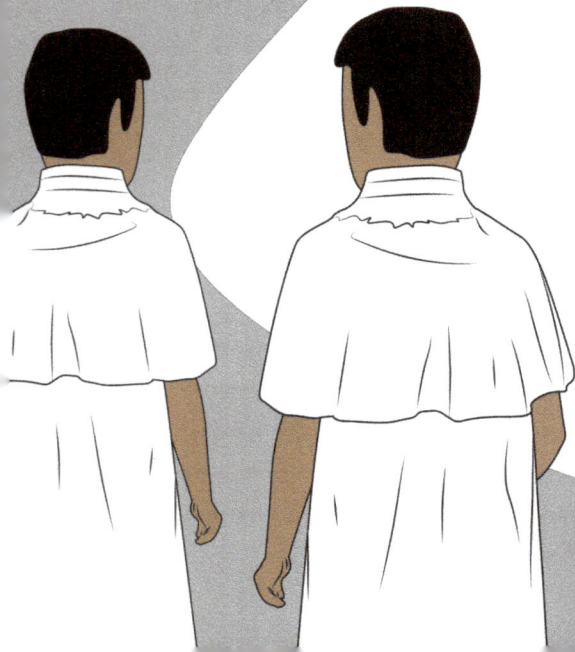

Even the children's choir was great! My brothers sang in the Treble Choir, and they sang all over the city. Christmas carols at City Hall, and concerts at different churches. My father drove us there in our faithful green station wagon that always had enough room to carry several other choir members along with us. I couldn't wait to join the choir! I eagerly anticipated the day when I would turn ten years old and be old enough to join, but I waited patiently because you had to be ten to join anything—even the Pathfinder Club. Since my brothers were in the choir, and the whole family went to all of the concerts, I knew all of the songs by heart. They sang so many concerts! No clapping was allowed in churches back then, but everyone would wave their programs in the air to show they liked the music. There were so much joy and satisfaction

in being in the presence of God in church and fellowshipping with other believers. Especially on the Sabbath when we stayed at church all day long.

The year 1969 came, and I turned nine years old! Only one more year to wait! Then my parents broke the news: "We're moving!" Fifth grade in a new school was so strange. Classes were held in a two-room schoolhouse known as "The Little School." None of the things I loved about Philadelphia existed in this country school. No double-dutch at recess time, no best friend, Audrey, none of the things I had waited so long to be a part of. No Treble Choir or Ebenezer Warriors Pathfinders. Not even

public transportation. I never thought I would miss riding the bus! At my new school, we had to walk a mile to school every day.

None of the things that kept my brothers busy in the city existed either; no wall ball or TOPS. Country life was boring! Now the focus of their attention somehow turned to other things. They managed to always find some mischief to get into. Desperately, my parents turned to music lessons. We each got to choose an instrument, and one evening a week, we were dropped off for our music lessons. This helped, but, of course, they continued to get into mischief. One morning at family worship, we discussed music: "How could sin begin in a perfect environment? Isn't heaven HEAVEN because no sin is there?" One of my brothers asked.

"Yes, that's why the devil was kicked out of heaven," my mother answered. "Let's read Ezekiel 28:13–15, 'Thou hast been in Eden the garden of God; every precious stone was thy covering, the sardius, topaz, and the diamond, the beryl, the onyx, and the jasper, the sapphire, the emerald, and the carbuncle, and gold: the workmanship of thy tabrets and of thy pipes was prepared in thee in the day that thou wast created. Thou art the anointed cherub that covereth; and I have set thee so: thou wast upon the holy mountain of God; thou hast walked up and down in the midst of the stones of fire. Thou wast perfect in thy ways from the day that thou wast created, till iniquity was found in thee.'

"One of these days, we can ask God face to face all about it, but for now, just remember that God has a plan of redemption! Let's read Revelation 21:1, which states, 'And I saw a new heaven and a new earth: for the first heaven and the first earth were passed away.'"

"So John, one of the twelve disciples of Jesus, who was exiled to the Isle of Patmos, saw the future in vision," exclaimed my oldest brother, Darryl.

"Exactly! John's vision of things to come involved worship in our future here on earth, and worship in the new heaven and earth."

"Can we read the Scriptures that say so?" I asked.

"We sure can," exclaimed my parents. So we read Revelation 13:15–17: "As many as would not worship the image of the beast should be killed. And he causeth all, both small and great, rich and poor, free and bond, to receive a mark in their right hand, or in their foreheads: And that no man might buy or sell, save he that had the mark, or name of the beast, or the number of his name.'"

"That sounds like Daniel 3!" my next oldest brother, Wesley, retorted.

"And coming in our day! 'And he was in vision on the Sabbath Day!" (see Rev. 1:10), said my third oldest brother, Alan.

We closed worship by reading Isaiah 66:22–23. "For as the new heavens and the new earth, which I will make, shall remain before me, saith the Lord, so shall your seed and your name remain. And it shall come to pass, that from one new moon to another, and from one sabbath to another, shall all flesh come to worship before me, saith the Lord." So family worship kept us all rooted and grounded in Bible promises, for the most part.

Daddy was a settling influence as well, but like all teenagers, if Daddy weren't home, my brothers would manage to get into some kind of mischief. Or, out came that "worldly music" that was not permitted when my parents were home.

"Let's put on some music," said my oldest brother.

"Yeah, crank up the stereo full-blast!" said my next oldest brother. Darryl had several stacks of 45s, and he would pull out his saxophone, put on his hat just like the one his favorite celebrity wore, and play and sway to the music.

"I'm going to be a famous musician," he said.

> **"Yeah, crank up the stereo full-blast!"**

"Here comes Daddy!" I yelled.

Immediately, the needle was ejected, records collected, and the only "beat" to be heard was that of feet scurrying down the hall. They made sure to keep that record collection away from Daddy! They knew that if he saw that music, each record would be taken from them, and broken into pieces!

Wesley played the tuba. His practice sessions were spent playing gospel favorites like Spiritual Rhapsody— a compilation of Negro spirituals. They were oldies but goodies, just like those old 33 1/3 rpm records on which they were recorded. My brother could blast that tuba loud enough to shake every pane in the big bay window in the living room, and in all the windows in the house, for that matter! He was quite capable of being the entire tuba section (which he was anyway) in our high school band at Pine Forge Academy. The only thing louder than my brother's tuba playing was his car stereo when he played eight-track tapes in his metallic blue 1964 Chevy. He and his friends surely put that tape player to the test as they sped along from state to state with their favorite music blasting away in their eardrums. This was when his "wild side" came out.

My third oldest brother was known as a great musician extraordinaire. "Practice band music?" he exclaimed quite frequently. "I already know my part!"

"I'm going to be a famous musician!" exclaimed yet another brother.

After two years of playing the trumpet in the school band, my aspiring-to-fame brother switched to the baritone horn the next year, and finally to the tuba in his senior year. He was now the lone tuba player, taking my recently-graduated older brother's place. This musical genius would tape songs from the radio and learn all of the instrumental parts by listening to them over and over again on my cassette tape recorder.

"Mom!" I yelled, "I want my cassette tape recorder back!"

"That is hers, so you just give it back, and do it now before I have to tell your daddy," mom would command. He always gave it back, but he was not happy about it.

Monday and Wednesday nights were band rehearsal, but Tuesdays and Thursdays were choir rehearsal. My fourth oldest brother wanted to play the flute, but no matter how he blew it, all he got was air.

WHOOO … WHOOO … WHOOO … WHOOO … No music at all. We all fell out laughing and teasing him when we got home.

"I quit!" he shouted.

"Keep practicing," said our music teacher. "It's only been a month."

But Dean never became a band member; he had another talent, though. He was a strong tenor voice in the Pine Forge Academy Choir all four years of high school.

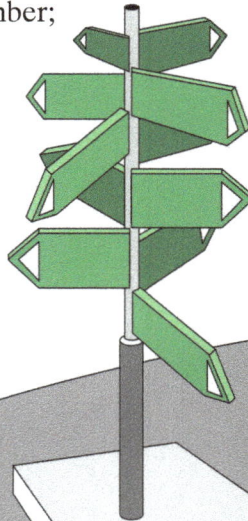

The choir/band tour every year during spring break was always the hot topic of conversation. "Are you going on tour?" was the question of the day, as we eagerly anticipated the posting of the list each year, giving us the opportunity to travel and see so many other places.

Luckily through it all, God's love remained consistent. Hebrews 13:5, "I will never leave thee, nor forsake thee," surely proved true through all of the crazy times of laughter, teasing, worldly music, and every aspect of high school. Another Bible promise that settled in my soul when I was young is found in Isaiah 58:13–14. "If thou turn away thy foot from the sabbath, from doing thy pleasure on my holy day; and call the sabbath a delight, the holy of the Lord, honourable; and shalt honor him, not doing thine own ways, nor finding thine own pleasure, nor speaking thine own words: Then shalt thou delight thyself in the Lord; and I will cause thee to ride upon the high places of the earth, and feed thee with the heritage of Jacob thy father: for the mouth of the Lord has spoken it."

Looking forward to the new earth that John saw in the book of Revelation, I see *Musicians Extraordinaire* around the throne, all singing and playing

> *Through it all, God's love remained consistent.*

instruments! "And I saw as it were a sea of glass mingled with fire: and them that had gotten the victory over the beast, and over his name, stand on the sea of glass, having harps of God Andy they sing the song of Moses and the Lamb" (Revelation 15: 1–2).

Looking back at my teen years, my brothers and I loved music. Another thing that was a constant in my life growing up was when we got together every Friday night at sunset, and all of the family would come together to open the Sabbath with my mom playing the piano. Those grand old hymns hold a special place in our hearts. "Don't forget the Sabbath, the Lord our God has blessed—Don't forget the Sabbath!" Always the record cabinet would be opened up, and all of the albums like the Blendwrights, The Ebenezer Sanctuary Choir, and even our own Pine Forge Academy Choir and Band albums would be stacked on the record player. Mom would join us in singing with her beautiful alto voice, and Dean, with his strong tenor voice, and myself, and the rest of my brothers playing instruments, would sing and play along. "Join us, please, Dad?" we cried.

"NO!" was always his answer. "But I'm listening, and I like what I hear!" he stated. "I love to buy the albums, and this is *always* the best day of the week!"

WAYS TO MAKE THE SABBATH THE BEST DAY OF THE WEEK!

- Iron your clothes, find matching bags and shoes, and have your entire outfit ready before Sabbath morning. No stress! You can make it to Sabbath School on time to enjoy songs and stories, and share in the discussion of the Sabbath School lesson!
- Open the Sabbath with praise and thanksgiving, recite Psalm 100, and serve the Lord with gladness!
- Play and sing praise music and songs!
- Memorize Scriptures!

> *Open the Sabbath with praise and thanksgiving.*

- Play Bible games, charades, and activities, encouraging all to use their talents, skills, and creativity to the glory and honor of God!
- Listen for keywords or phrases throughout the sermon making tally marks each time those words or phrases are heard and reward small gifts or tokens to whoever has the most, and then discuss during Sabbath dinner!
- Enhance the dinner table with fresh flowers!
- Make favorite foods and desserts for Sabbath dinner!
- Have a special toy box for younger children with toys only to be played with on Sabbath to make them special!
- Take nature walks/hikes after Sabbath dinner!
- Find objects out in nature, and tell why you chose it and how it pertains to the Sabbath or Sabbath sermon.
- Invite guests home for Sabbath dinner such as friends for the younger children; have every age of your family represented, and invite guests home so you can get to know someone new. Play Sabbath sermons and videos to discuss together!
- Always repeat the affirmation of our faith together, which is found in Exodus 20:8–11, "Remember the Sabbath day to keep it holy!"
- Study Bible prophecy, especially the books of Daniel and Revelation, to prepare for the end times and the second coming of Jesus!

www.ingramcontent.com/pod-product-compliance
Lightning Source LLC
Chambersburg PA
CBHW050824090426
42738CB00020B/3470